SCHIRMER'S LIBRARY
OF MUSICAL CLASSICS

Vol. 816

PETER I. TSCHAIKOWSKY

Op. 39

Album for the Young

Twenty-Four Easy Piano-Pieces

Edited and Fingered by

ADOLF RUTHARDT

Translations by

DR. THEODORE BAKER

G. SCHIRMER, Inc.

DISTRIBUTED BY

HAL•LEONARD®
CORPORATION

7777 W. BLUEMOUND RD. P.O. BOX 13819 MILWAUKEE, WI 53213

Album for the Young.

1. Morning Prayer.

P. TSCHAIKOWSKY. Op.39.

2. A Winter Morning.

3. The Hobby-horse.

4. Mamma.

5. March of the Tin Soldiers.

Tempo di Marcia.

6. The Sick Doll.

7. The Doll's Burial.

8. Waltz.

9. The New Doll.

10. Mazurka.

Tempo di Mazurka.

11. Russian Song.

12. The Peasant Plays the Accordion.

13. Folk-song.

Comodo.

14. Polka.

15. Italian Song.

16. Old French Song.

Moderato assai.

17. German Song.

18. Neapolitan Dance-song.

19. The Nurse's Tale.

20. The Witch.

21. Sweet Dreams

P. I. Tchaikovsky, Op. 39, No. 21

17224

28

22. Song of the Lark.

23. The Handorgan Man.

24. In Church.